girl

A REFLECTION OF THE COMING-OF-AGE OF A YOUNG GIRL THROUGH POETRY

LEE GIFFEN

Fulton Books, Inc.
Meadville, PA

Published by Fulton Books 2020

ISBN 978-1-64952-549-9 (paperback)
ISBN 978-1-64952-550-5 (digital)

Printed in the United States of America

Wrote these words so they could live outside my head a little. Dedicated to my parents who always saw the light in me when I failed to do so myself. As well as the people of New York City—the toughest people on the planet.

All my love, always, Lee.

The Beginning
of the End

The Beginning of the End

She was drunk—a tasteless blur of cheap wine and beer she didn't even like to drink. She was pretty, but the longer you stared, her eyes looked more sad rather than green.

The garage door was opened all the way, but the summer air made it feel as if they were sitting on the sun itself. The girl was well-known only for bad reasons, had lots of friends, and never seemed to be alone. However, she always felt painfully alone. She had the type of friends most parents would hate. Later on, she learned to hate them too.

The longer she sat on the garage floor that sticky night, looking at the company she was surrounded with, she realized her potential was slipping from her. It had slipped so greatly she began to hate herself.

An oversize baseball jacket she stole from her dad's closet draped over her legs and caused beads of sweat to drip down the back of her thighs. Shorts rolled up, for reasons she now would be embarrassed to admit, caught the attention of those who didn't deserve to watch. A stack of bracelets dangled on her left arm every time she would tug on her necklaces nervously.

She watched the others act foolishly, intoxicated from things no one should have access to. She saw them get sad when it ran out. She became sad with them. She watched the endless cycle of the same results. The girls were cruel, and the boys were ignorant.

She was living a night she now wishes could be plucked from her brain and placed on the highest shelf somewhere in her kitchen. No one should have to live nights like how she lived hers. This was the beginning of her end.

The Struggle

THE YEARS OF GROWING

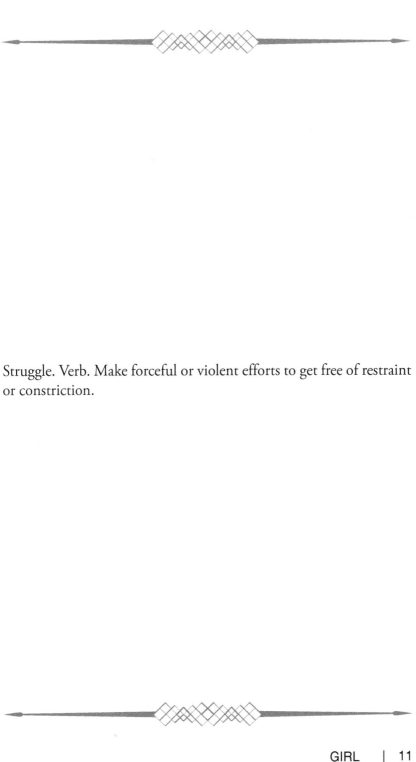

Struggle. Verb. Make forceful or violent efforts to get free of restraint or constriction.

She lay stretched out in the sand, eyes squinted and hair matted into a nest resting upon her shoulders. The ocean felt far away from her, but she lay several feet from it. She had a blinding headache, like splinters jabbing and twisting their way into the palm of a foot. The sway of the water back and forth was the most consistent thing her life knew.

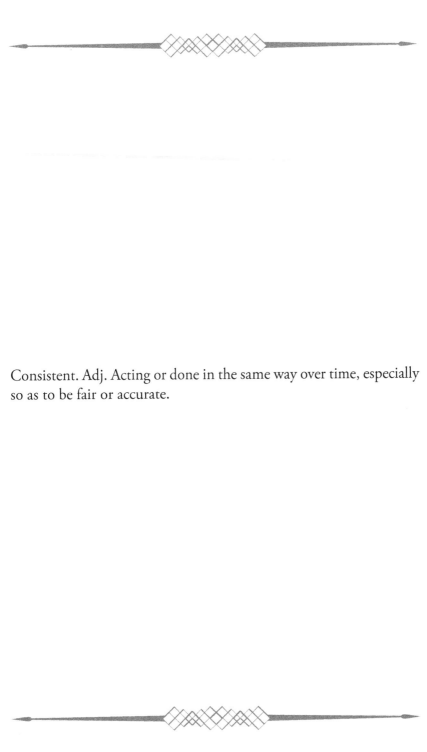

Consistent. Adj. Acting or done in the same way over time, especially so as to be fair or accurate.

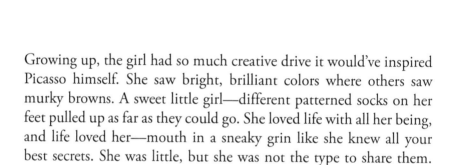

Growing up, the girl had so much creative drive it would've inspired Picasso himself. She saw bright, brilliant colors where others saw murky browns. A sweet little girl—different patterned socks on her feet pulled up as far as they could go. She loved life with all her being, and life loved her—mouth in a sneaky grin like she knew all your best secrets. She was little, but she was not the type to share them. Gave the tightest hugs and laughed louder than anyone on the block. Her parents wondered how they got so lucky.

A constant ringing in her ears.

She wished for better days. A colorful mess she was. Her dreams locked away in haze. Negativity around her consumed her very being. Angry words and sharp tones made her bones feel lazy. Her ears still ring sometimes.

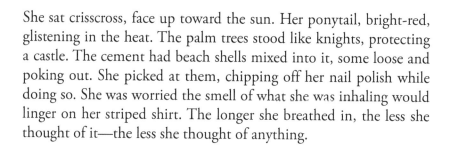

She sat crisscross, face up toward the sun. Her ponytail, bright-red, glistening in the heat. The palm trees stood like knights, protecting a castle. The cement had beach shells mixed into it, some loose and poking out. She picked at them, chipping off her nail polish while doing so. She was worried the smell of what she was inhaling would linger on her striped shirt. The longer she breathed in, the less she thought of it—the less she thought of anything.

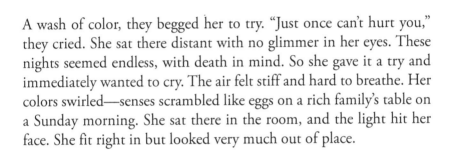

A wash of color, they begged her to try. "Just once can't hurt you," they cried. She sat there distant with no glimmer in her eyes. These nights seemed endless, with death in mind. So she gave it a try and immediately wanted to cry. The air felt stiff and hard to breathe. Her colors swirled—senses scrambled like eggs on a rich family's table on a Sunday morning. She sat there in the room, and the light hit her face. She fit right in but looked very much out of place.

A circle of thoughts ran through her head as she gathered in the group. The boys and girls hated one other. Harsh words and lies said only to backbones—all dressed in the same uniform of pretending to be what they were not.

No one had hopes. And no one had dreams. She thought this is what life was.

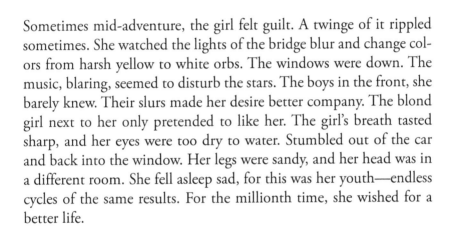

Sometimes mid-adventure, the girl felt guilt. A twinge of it rippled sometimes. She watched the lights of the bridge blur and change colors from harsh yellow to white orbs. The windows were down. The music, blaring, seemed to disturb the stars. The boys in the front, she barely knew. Their slurs made her desire better company. The blond girl next to her only pretended to like her. The girl's breath tasted sharp, and her eyes were too dry to water. Stumbled out of the car and back into the window. Her legs were sandy, and her head was in a different room. She fell asleep sad, for this was her youth—endless cycles of the same results. For the millionth time, she wished for a better life.

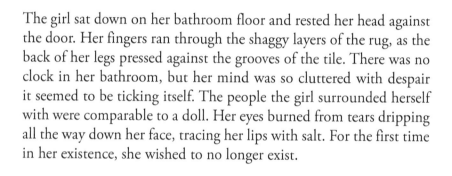

The girl sat down on her bathroom floor and rested her head against the door. Her fingers ran through the shaggy layers of the rug, as the back of her legs pressed against the grooves of the tile. There was no clock in her bathroom, but her mind was so cluttered with despair it seemed to be ticking itself. The people the girl surrounded herself with were comparable to a doll. Her eyes burned from tears dripping all the way down her face, tracing her lips with salt. For the first time in her existence, she wished to no longer exist.

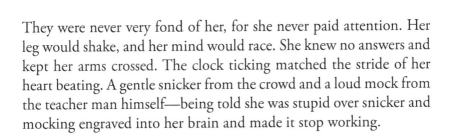

They were never very fond of her, for she never paid attention. Her leg would shake, and her mind would race. She knew no answers and kept her arms crossed. The clock ticking matched the stride of her heart beating. A gentle snicker from the crowd and a loud mock from the teacher man himself—being told she was stupid over snicker and mocking engraved into her brain and made it stop working.

The girl was filled with bad habits—her mouth spewing lies about where she really was. Her emotions were so tangled her eight-hour days of clock-ticking became one of the most draining things for her to endure. The boy who sat next to her in class often reminded her of *the* boy who only liked seeing her in the moonlight. The girl, at the time, was a bad friend. She was selfish. Only cared about looking cool and kissing even cooler boys with her salty lips. She was a puzzle. Or perhaps, she was similar to a board game that one would be forced to play while visiting their grandparents—pieces missing, cards ripped, instructions lost years ago, a game no one liked to play. The girl was a colorful, rotten mess.

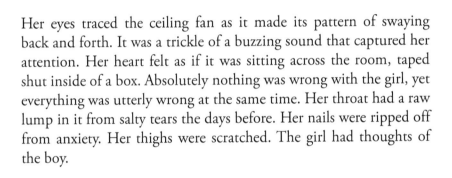

Her eyes traced the ceiling fan as it made its pattern of swaying back and forth. It was a trickle of a buzzing sound that captured her attention. Her heart felt as if it was sitting across the room, taped shut inside of a box. Absolutely nothing was wrong with the girl, yet everything was utterly wrong at the same time. Her throat had a raw lump in it from salty tears the days before. Her nails were ripped off from anxiety. Her thighs were scratched. The girl had thoughts of the boy.

The girl sat in front of the toilet and gazed into the face looking back at her. The distorted image looked nothing like the girl. But at this moment, the girl had no idea who she was anymore. The substances bubbled inside of her, making her mouth warm, her arms loose, and legs numb. She wanted her insides to come out. Teardrops fled onto the seat as the girl let out a loud cry. Her palms tightened around her neck, and her eyes began to see tiny black stars. The girl locked eyes with the reflection. She wanted to be skinny.

Life seemed like a pool. She was not a fast swimmer.

Only young once—youth filled her body like blood. Her bones were made of resistance, her hair strands of rebellion, her eyes cloudy windows into her dreams, her legs carrying her into mistakes, her arms carrying her into regret. Her heart matched the stride of others around her. Her youth was exactly what it shouldn't be. She was so young, and her soul was so tired.

She sat in the front seat of a car. She was told someone had called her a nobody. The sentence echoed over and over so loud it screamed in her head, bounced until it started to ring. She will never forget the feeling. She already felt next to nothing. It just felt too real now.

The girl longed to be loved. No matter where she looked, she never fit in. The options were slim already. But most considered her weird. So this made the options even slimmer. The girl was made fun of for the way she spoke. It was a soft, slow way the words tumbled out from her lips, almost like she examined each word before letting it leave her brain. The way they made fun of her, carefully placing her name before each harsh remark, made her talk less.

So the tumble of her slow words wouldn't cause boys to mimic. She began to hate the sound of her name, for what came after made her tears tumble instead of words. The girl longed for her pain to stop.

If you were a song, I wish for you to never be played. If you were a book, I wish for you to never be written. If you were a toy, I wish for no one to play with you. If you were a cup of coffee, I wish for everyone to order tea. If you were a kite, I wish for your strings to get tangled. If you were a shadow, I wish for someone to turn on the light. If you still have memories of me, I wish for you to forget them. For I no longer play your song.

Was the girl hard for him to love? For she wants your mind, but you miss her body. For she misses your smile, but you miss her touch. For she wants to hear your laugh, but you want late nights with her. For she wants to listen to all words spoken from your tongue, but you want to turn the music higher. If she could show you her heart before she met you, it would be a bright, brilliant color of red and fantastic pinks. Now it is faded to a confused puddle of purple. She would never give you the honor of destroying her as a person, but she gave you the gift of killing all her love to give. She wishes to never love like that again.

A late spring night hugged the air as the girl lay wide-awake—backbone bent into the mattress, lips salty, eyes puffy. The boy called for her to join him, for he only enjoyed her presence under moonlight. The thought of him made her sobs destroy her rib cage. While her lungs wither into nothingness, she looked into her reflection across the room. Her eyes hadn't looked green in quite some time. She dressed herself and climbed out into the moonlight to meet the boy who never wished to see her in the sun. She was worried her lips tasted of salt.

Love is a strange thing. It's so powerful and infinite. It destroys people. It builds people. It's the most overwhelming thing one can experience.

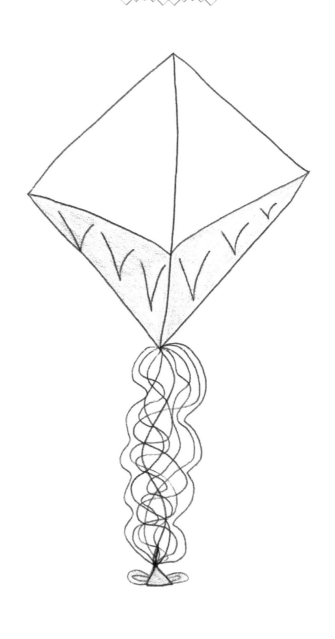

His lips dripped of honey like on a summer day. Left a smirk on his face as he laughed at the girl. She wanted his love. He never listened to the words that fell from her mouth. He loved her for reasons other than her mind. She lay her head, resting on the passenger-side window. She had a sneaky grin like she knew all his secrets. She, this time, knew his secret. He would never love a girl like her. This was a secret she kept to herself.

An intense confusion of your name bubbles through my head. You are the sweetest bitter taste my mouth has ever tasted.

Her past with him stayed, helped her fight harder to have better. It left her burned—a warm flame through her heart.

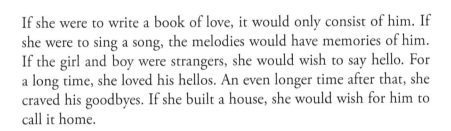

If she were to write a book of love, it would only consist of him. If she were to sing a song, the melodies would have memories of him. If the girl and boy were strangers, she would wish to say hello. For a long time, she loved his hellos. An even longer time after that, she craved his goodbyes. If she built a house, she would wish for him to call it home.

Jealousy rotted her heart.

She was so jealous of everything around him—the people he spoke to every day, the people that made him laugh. Jealous of the stars that got to watch him. Jealous of the sun always touching him. Jealous of gravity for holding him down when she never could. She always would love him.

She would never trust him. For nothing made her smile harder. For nothing made her cry harder than him.

A crowded room full of people who were nothing but cruel. Their words battled like a wizards' duel. The way they all acted caused the walls to turn away. If the girl were to be a bird, she would like to fly very far away. Ridicule and thick smoke bombarded the air. She looked at her hands and seemed to not care. Lazy exhales across the room made the people less cruel.

Her nervousness felt contagious as if she touched another soul. They too would fall under the dizzy spell of always being in a fuss.

A numb feeling from the smallest hairs on the top of her head all the way down to her pinkie toes. Her cheeks are rosy, followed by a smile more frozen than a doll. She blamed herself for the frozen feeling, for it never seemed to go away. And she doesn't remember when it arrived.

The bell echoed through the building followed by an obnoxious grumble of children walking. The girl stood stiff like a weed in grass, her hands cupped over her eyes.

A warm liquid seeped from the corner of her eyes, down to her pinkie toes.

A second bell echoed. She was fragile. She was frozen.

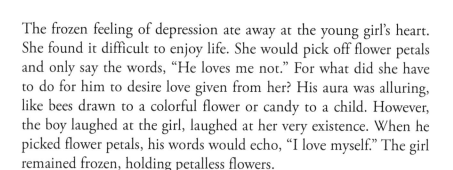

The frozen feeling of depression ate away at the young girl's heart. She found it difficult to enjoy life. She would pick off flower petals and only say the words, "He loves me not." For what did she have to do for him to desire love given from her? His aura was alluring, like bees drawn to a colorful flower or candy to a child. However, the boy laughed at the girl, laughed at her very existence. When he picked flower petals, his words would echo, "I love myself." The girl remained frozen, holding petalless flowers.

A rush to get ready and make believe she was pretty to impress people that didn't deserve to be impressed. A smear of color under her eyes patted over again and again with a brush. Mascara clumps fell under her eyes from last night's waterfalls—glitter above and below, darker colors in certain places. She looked at her reflection in the mirror. Her red hair now sat below her chin, too short to tie up. She didn't want to leave her bathroom. She didn't want to hear bells echo all day and listen to other people's songs. She wished for a different face.

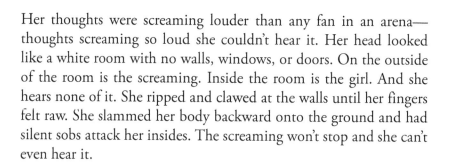

Her thoughts were screaming louder than any fan in an arena—thoughts screaming so loud she couldn't hear it. Her head looked like a white room with no walls, windows, or doors. On the outside of the room is the screaming. Inside the room is the girl. And she hears none of it. She ripped and clawed at the walls until her fingers felt raw. She slammed her body backward onto the ground and had silent sobs attack her insides. The screaming won't stop and she can't even hear it.

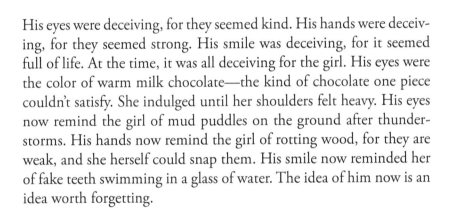

His eyes were deceiving, for they seemed kind. His hands were deceiving, for they seemed strong. His smile was deceiving, for it seemed full of life. At the time, it was all deceiving for the girl. His eyes were the color of warm milk chocolate—the kind of chocolate one piece couldn't satisfy. She indulged until her shoulders felt heavy. His eyes now remind the girl of mud puddles on the ground after thunderstorms. His hands now remind the girl of rotting wood, for they are weak, and she herself could snap them. His smile now reminded her of fake teeth swimming in a glass of water. The idea of him now is an idea worth forgetting.

A sore sight to some—she saw beauty and grace. She thanked the stars, and it made her feel special. He was a love so great. She was not great enough to receive the love. He reminded her of the ocean. Chaos made her calm. He was her chaos.

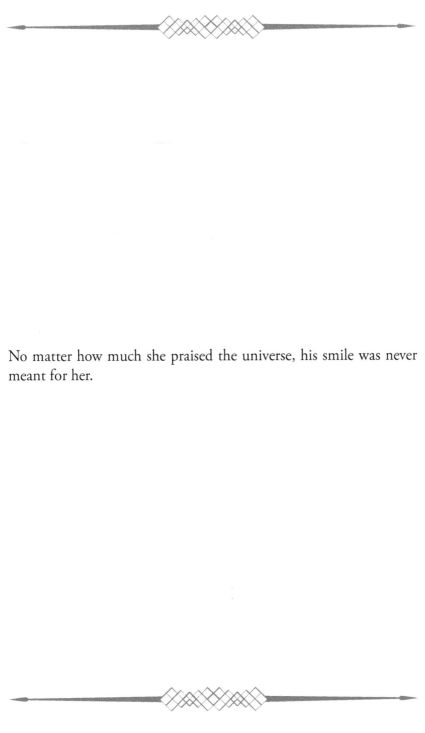

No matter how much she praised the universe, his smile was never meant for her.

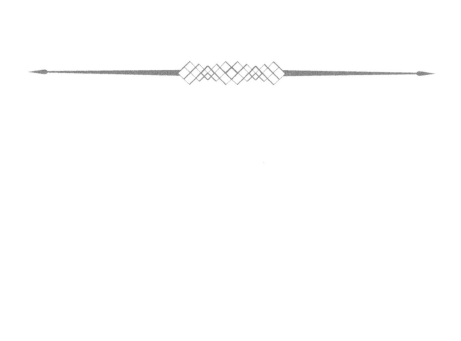

Universe. N. All existing matter and space considered as a whole, the cosmos.

The way he presented himself was quite misleading. His brown eyes were kind and so gentle. He was pretty enough to be someone's archangel. A stench followed him. Arrogance made his locks look greasy. His ego stained his clothes. Some looked up to him. Some girls idolized him for reasons no one could explain. A label, "poisoned," could've been written in the most beautiful French across his face, and the girl still would've drunk anyway. She loved the idea of him. She loved the thought of him. Poison made her stomach hurt and made her thoughts cloud. Overtime, she wished she had never come into the existence of the boy with the brown eyes.

She really loved him in a bizarre way. For it was a pair that should never be paired together. It was like wearing a sandal and a sneaker at the same time. It was like driving a car with no wheels. It was like loving someone who doesn't love you back. He was destroying her. Yet he was the muse.

Archangel. N. An angel of high rank

The girl was struggling. She herself was a struggle. Couldn't focus on life. Had pieces missing from her puzzle. Had her shoes untied, buttons that needed buttoning, hair that needed brushing, clothes needing patching, lungs needing fresh air.

Her mind needed clarity—hopes that needed to be hopeful. Arms that needed to be held. She had dreams that needed to be dreamed. She was trying so desperately to grow flowers on the path she was on. She wished for them to bloom one day. She wished for the struggle to stop.

The Sun

THE STOPPING OF
THE STRUGGLE

Sun. N. The star around which the earth orbits.

If I reached out and wished to hold your hand,
I wish for your hand to always be there. If you have dreams,
I wish to know of them. For I could dream with you.

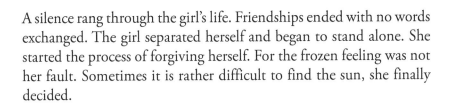

A silence rang through the girl's life. Friendships ended with no words exchanged. The girl separated herself and began to stand alone. She started the process of forgiving herself. For the frozen feeling was not her fault. Sometimes it is rather difficult to find the sun, she finally decided.

The pain of old memories, the girl placed in an imaginary fireplace. A wise woman told her to not forget her mistakes, instead to blossom from them and learn. However, the pain of holding on to some memories was too great for the girl. The ringing of name-calling and embarrassment, the girl dropped into the fireplace. She watched the memories trickle across the wood and burst into flame. She wished for the boy that caused her so much sadness to find a girl one day—a girl that would give him everything she never did. She hoped he would call her pretty and how the universe balances around her. She loved him so much. She wished for him to be happy. The girl watched his name burn in the flames.

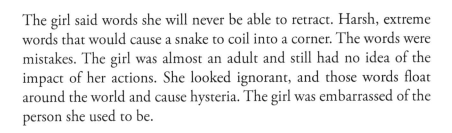

The girl said words she will never be able to retract. Harsh, extreme words that would cause a snake to coil into a corner. The words were mistakes. The girl was almost an adult and still had no idea of the impact of her actions. She looked ignorant, and those words float around the world and cause hysteria. The girl was embarrassed of the person she used to be.

No matter how much the girl loved life, sometimes she would lay awake in the hours of the moonlight. Her thoughts troubled her, and nerves would bend her to her core. Life felt heavy on these nights, almost like she was where she used to exist. Her body felt a part of her bed.

The silent tears that swept down her face came from a place of putting so much pressure on herself. The girl wished for the pain to stop. The pain liked to come back sometimes.

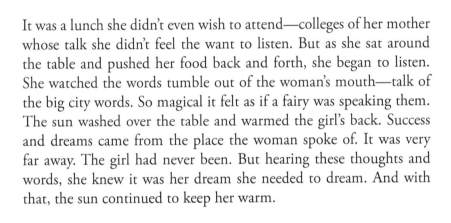

It was a lunch she didn't even wish to attend—colleges of her mother whose talk she didn't feel the want to listen. But as she sat around the table and pushed her food back and forth, she began to listen. She watched the words tumble out of the woman's mouth—talk of the big city words. So magical it felt as if a fairy was speaking them. The sun washed over the table and warmed the girl's back. Success and dreams came from the place the woman spoke of. It was very far away. The girl had never been. But hearing these thoughts and words, she knew it was her dream she needed to dream. And with that, the sun continued to keep her warm.

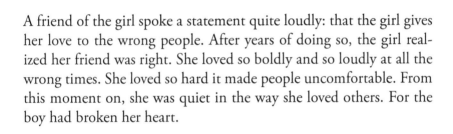

A friend of the girl spoke a statement quite loudly: that the girl gives her love to the wrong people. After years of doing so, the girl realized her friend was right. She loved so boldly and so loudly at all the wrong times. She loved so hard it made people uncomfortable. From this moment on, she was quiet in the way she loved others. For the boy had broken her heart.

Life is full of losses and gains. Some are harder than others—some that make you question life itself.

Gains are easy. They make life float beneath your feet and bring happiness to the most important aspects of life. Losses are crippling and hard to understand at the time they happen.

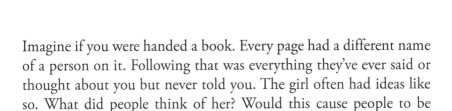

Imagine if you were handed a book. Every page had a different name of a person on it. Following that was everything they've ever said or thought about you but never told you. The girl often had ideas like so. What did people think of her? Would this cause people to be kinder to others?

She wanted to make the world a beautiful place—to completely rid the struggle from her, to have her flowers bloom. She had thoughts of the city.

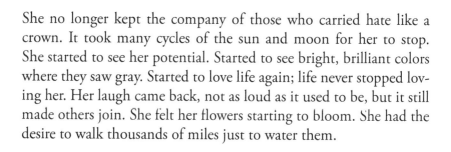

She no longer kept the company of those who carried hate like a crown. It took many cycles of the sun and moon for her to stop. She started to see her potential. Started to see bright, brilliant colors where they saw gray. Started to love life again; life never stopped loving her. Her laugh came back, not as loud as it used to be, but it still made others join. She felt her flowers starting to bloom. She had the desire to walk thousands of miles just to water them.

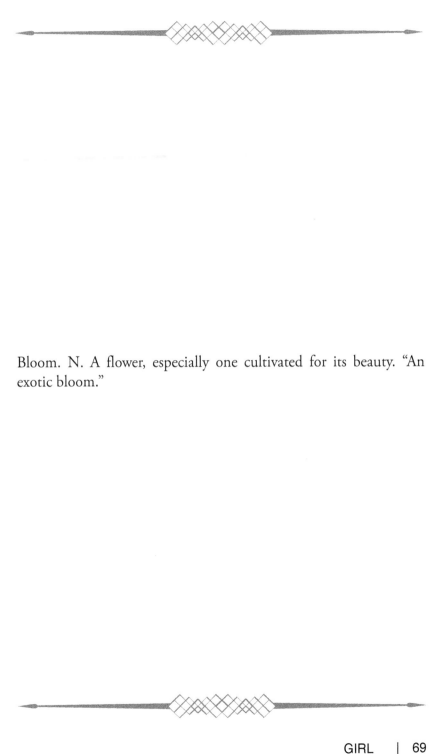

Bloom. N. A flower, especially one cultivated for its beauty. "An exotic bloom."

A notebook began to fill of future adventures, none which consisted of blurry car rides with lack of good company—adventures of creative drive, enough to make Picasso himself jealous.

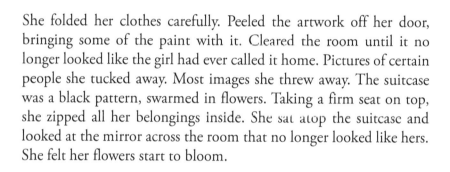

She folded her clothes carefully. Peeled the artwork off her door, bringing some of the paint with it. Cleared the room until it no longer looked like the girl had ever called it home. Pictures of certain people she tucked away. Most images she threw away. The suitcase was a black pattern, swarmed in flowers. Taking a firm seat on top, she zipped all her belongings inside. She sat atop the suitcase and looked at the mirror across the room that no longer looked like hers. She felt her flowers start to bloom.

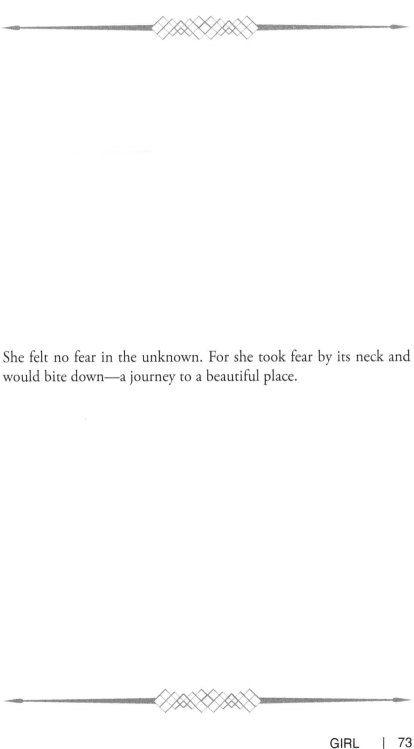

She felt no fear in the unknown. For she took fear by its neck and would bite down—a journey to a beautiful place.

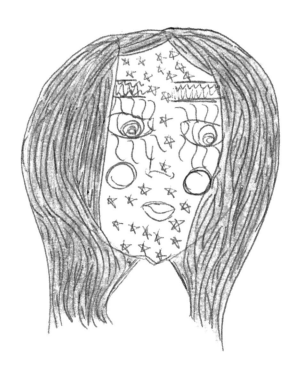

The City

THE END OF THE BEGINNING

City. N. A large town

The girl had lived in the city for two days. There were little to no words to describe the joy she had come to know—the happiest she had been in all her lifetimes.

She was on a walk in late October. The constant hum of the people around her matched with the stride of her heartbeat.

She was walking with leaps that landed so gracefully it could put a ballerina to shame.

She entered a café and placed her order. The cashier asked what inspired her outfit. The girl raised a grin like she knew all his best secrets. She replied loftily, saying she always looked as so. He seemed taken aback at first. She had what seemed like millions of patterns covering her.

From the hairs on the top of her head down to her pinkie toes, he asked what she wanted to do in life. The girl paused and then answered him.

The art she created, she saw her past and present. The swirls of the colors, the combinations of paint, charcoal, and pencil brought life to pages and kept her life afloat. She is art.

The city air made the girl feel powerful, beyond it. She felt she ruled it. She felt protected by the energy that encircled it. It made her tough.

Tougher than she had ever been. Tough from the top of her hair all the way down to her pinkie toes.

She was walking on her way to the train as a little girl ran up to her with a camera in hand. The little girl seemed timid as her mom stood several feet behind her. A question was proposed to take a picture of the girl. For her style was so unique. The little girl was building a project on people of the city. Flattered, the picture was taken.

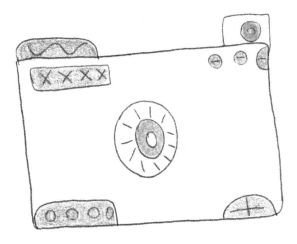

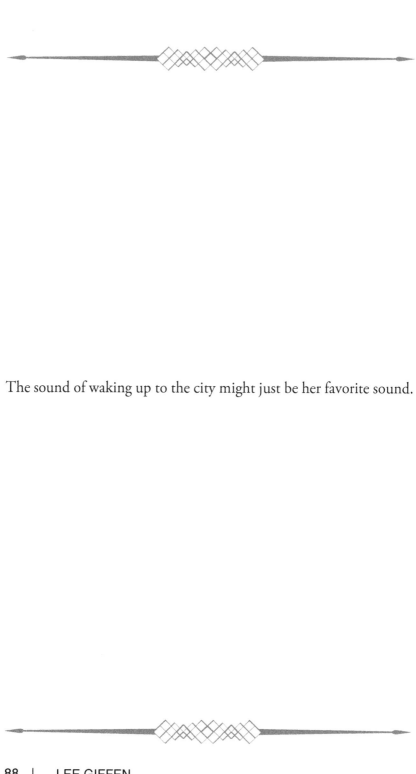

The sound of waking up to the city might just be her favorite sound.

The girl took a seat on the train and observed around her like she always did. A woman sat across from her and, quite possibly, was the strangest being to ever walk this earth—striking resemblance of a bird. Her shoes consisted of no socks while the palms of her feet rested on the train floor, where splinters could easily jam their way in. She held a muffin in her hand. The side of her face received more muffin than her mouth.

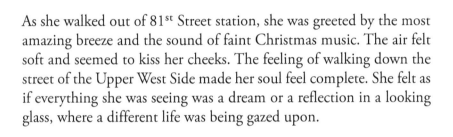

As she walked out of 81st Street station, she was greeted by the most amazing breeze and the sound of faint Christmas music. The air felt soft and seemed to kiss her cheeks. The feeling of walking down the street of the Upper West Side made her soul feel complete. She felt as if everything she was seeing was a dream or a reflection in a looking glass, where a different life was being gazed upon.

Looking glass. N. A mirror

The girl felt embarrassed for the woman on the train today. The woman was riled up and spewing angry, harsh words like she was being paid to do so. She was homeless for sure—on some sort of drug that made her mad at the world. Guilt filled the girl to the brim. Drugs are a horrible, horrible thing. Her body resembles a raisin, how shriveled it was—her knees knobby and her eyes sunken in. She seemed like she used to be really pretty. Maybe she used to be really smart. Used to have potential. But on this cold November night, she was angry at the world, and the world was choosing not to listen.

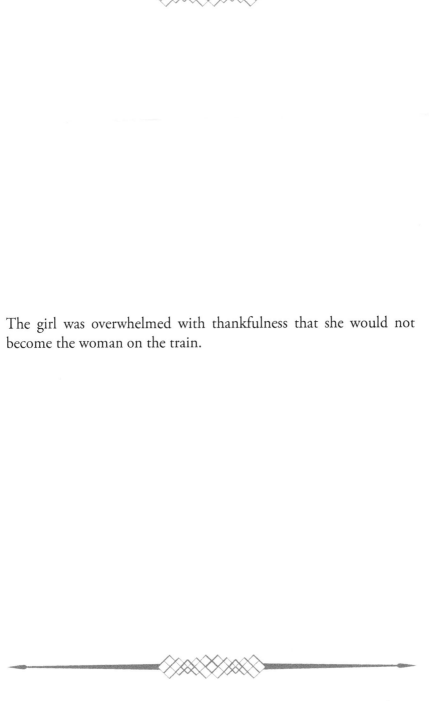

The girl was overwhelmed with thankfulness that she would not become the woman on the train.

She loved that city so much she'd die for it. She gave her life so that the city could breathe life into others. It gave her hope. Made her wild in all the best ways. Made her grow into the person she's always meant to be.

Her flowers continued to bloom.

A certain beauty was held inside her—a graceful energy where she felt light. Her feet walked faster than her mind could carry her. She had no time to sleep in this city. It seemed to be one of the rules. Every ounce of her felt a part of the lights. Her life was magical. The beauty was always inside her. She just never looked. The city looked for her.

A train ride out of the city to the shore felt like the peak of the girl's existence. The air within the train felt a late summer breeze. The wind was giving her kisses. She wished she could ride forever.

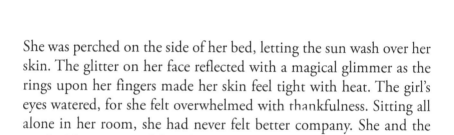

She was perched on the side of her bed, letting the sun wash over her skin. The glitter on her face reflected with a magical glimmer as the rings upon her fingers made her skin feel tight with heat. The girl's eyes watered, for she felt overwhelmed with thankfulness. Sitting all alone in her room, she had never felt better company. She and the sun had become good friends.

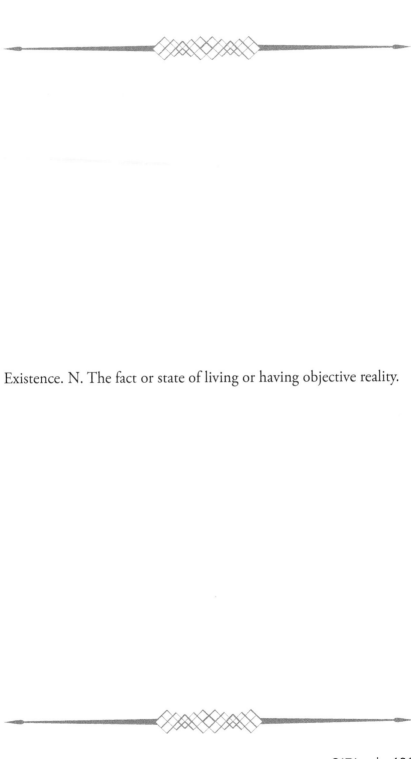

Existence. N. The fact or state of living or having objective reality.

The girl would observe people on the train and give them stories in her head. She wondered who they loved the most on earth. What helped them get up every day.

If they loved the city as much as she did., if they had ever felt frozen, or if they ever felt the sun was soaking into their skin. She wondered if they wondered about her. The girl with a million secrets riding the train somewhere in her city.

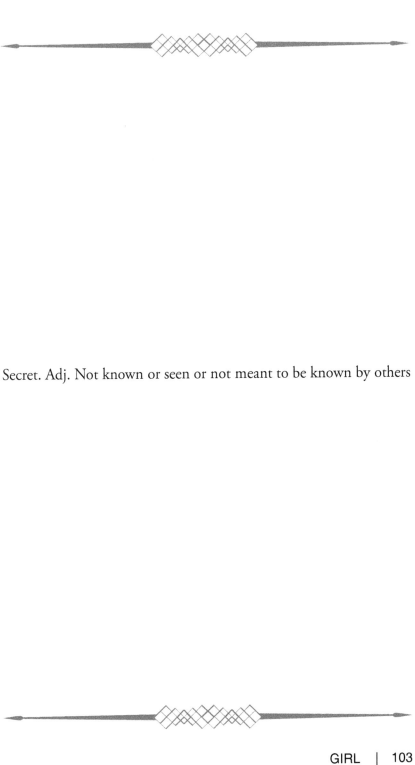

Secret. Adj. Not known or seen or not meant to be known by others

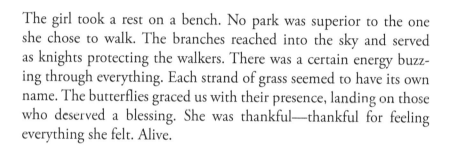

The girl took a rest on a bench. No park was superior to the one she chose to walk. The branches reached into the sky and served as knights protecting the walkers. There was a certain energy buzzing through everything. Each strand of grass seemed to have its own name. The butterflies graced us with their presence, landing on those who deserved a blessing. She was thankful—thankful for feeling everything she felt. Alive.

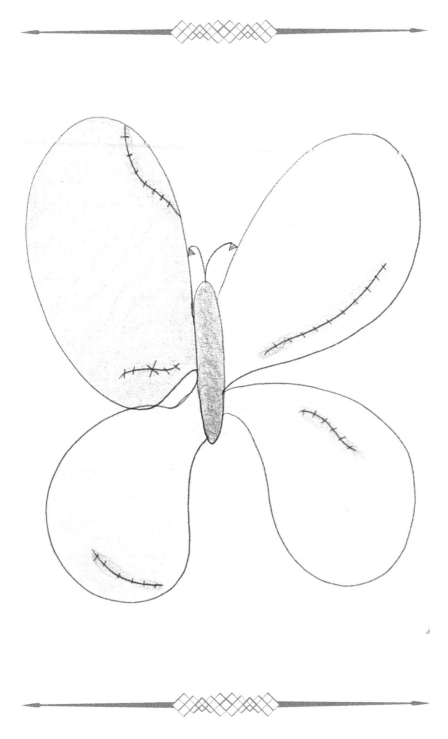

The most beautiful thing in the world was to unconditionally be yourself. The girl knew this, and she spoke these words to herself every day through the mirror. It took quite some time and mental energy to realize people will hate you when they see you succeed. The girl realized this but never understood it.

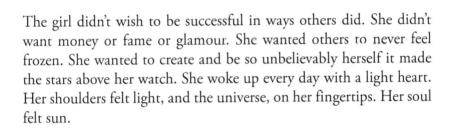

The girl didn't wish to be successful in ways others did. She didn't want money or fame or glamour. She wanted others to never feel frozen. She wanted to create and be so unbelievably herself it made the stars above her watch. She woke up every day with a light heart. Her shoulders felt light, and the universe, on her fingertips. Her soul felt sun.

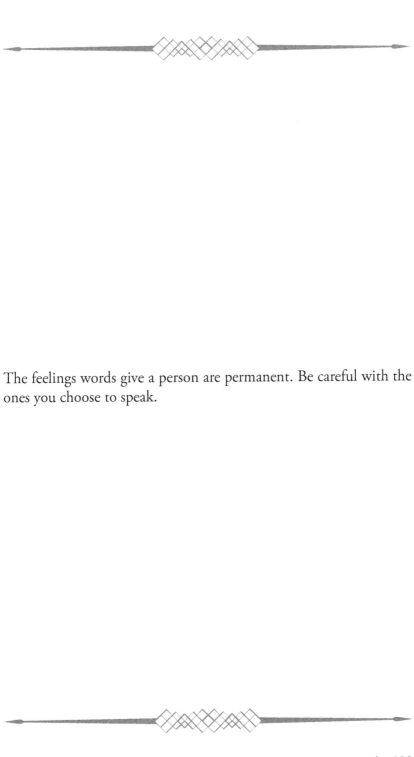

The feelings words give a person are permanent. Be careful with the ones you choose to speak.

There is a certain beauty in the girl's resilience—a type of beauty that swept her of her misery, a golden child wrecked in silver.

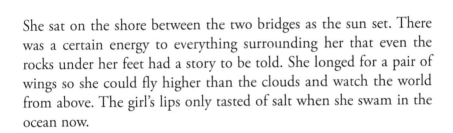

She sat on the shore between the two bridges as the sun set. There was a certain energy to everything surrounding her that even the rocks under her feet had a story to be told. She longed for a pair of wings so she could fly higher than the clouds and watch the world from above. The girl's lips only tasted of salt when she swam in the ocean now.

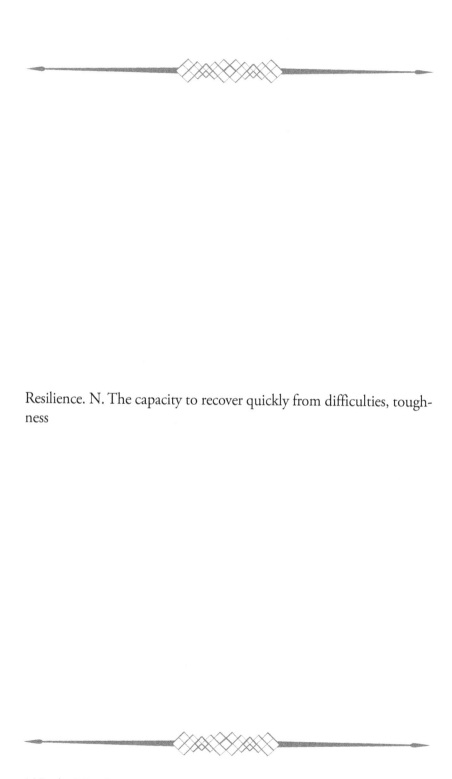

Resilience. N. The capacity to recover quickly from difficulties, tough-
ness

Living life without purpose is a life not worth living. Dream the wildest dreams—dreams so amazingly big they scare everyone. Bring love into everything. Love life, and life will never stop loving you.

Many stars above her watched the girl grow. The girl will always pretend the horribleness of her coming of age never happened. Tuck away the thoughts: she was never good enough. But her worth was known now. The stars sent her the sun so her frozen feeling would thaw. The stars graced her with train rides, walks in the most superior park in the world so her heartbeat could stop matching the strides of others. If she were to build a house, only she wishes to call it home. She took her struggle and turned it into something magical. The girl grew up. The woman was powerful.

About the Author

Lee Giffen is a New York City-based artist with a passion for writing and inspiring others. She believes art can impact people's lives in indescribable ways. A phrase you will often hear Lee say is "Everyone is art in their own way." If Lee could give anyone advice about life, it would be to be so unbelievably yourself it makes the world uncomfortable.

CPSIA information can be obtained
at www.ICGtesting.com
Printed in the USA
LVHW070228210221
679378LV00018BA/252

9 781649 525499